T0392320

The Trials and Tribulations Of Kittyhood

By:

Aphrodite Vasilas

To order additional copies of this book, contact:
Xlibris
844-714-8691
www.Xlibris.com
Orders@Xlibris.com

ISBN: Softcover   979-8-3694-2418-6
         EBook   979-8-3694-2417-9

Library of Congress Control Number: 2024912243

Print information available on the last page

Rev. date: 06/13/2024

This is dedicated to the most beautiful cat in the world. (Of course I'm prejudiced…)

Thank you to my human mommy for typing this for me. (My
paws didn't work too good on the keyboard.)

Chapter One

THE CAT AT THE DOOR

My name is Aphrodite. They tell me I am named after the Greek Goddess of Love. If I am supposed to be a "lover, not a fighter", it was never really explained to me. (But you can pass the theory along to any mice you run into….they won't be so inclined to run away from me….until it's too late.)

But…I am getting ahead of myself. What I really wanted to explain is how I became known as "The Cat at the Door!"

My mommy and daddy found this great shelter and I was brought into this world under the back porch of a mobile home. A few weeks later, I finally ventured out to see the world. Mommy and Daddy tried to explain to me about all the bad things that could happen and how careful I would have to be.

One of the first strange things I saw were these creatures that walked on two legs. Mommy told me that some of

Hera (also known as Mommy)

these creatures (they were called "humans") were nice and some were not so nice. These particular "humans" seemed to be of the nice variety. If I remember correctly, my mommy told me to go over and act 'cute'. They would fall in love with me and take care of us. Well, it worked, and it wasn't long until they started putting out food for us. After a short hesitation, Mommy went over and sniffed at the dish. Deciding it was OK, she helped herself. Daddy finally tried out the food, and finding it to his liking, dug in.

During the rest of the summer, Mommy (now named Hera) and Daddy (now named Zeus) kept a close eye on me, except when the two humans were near. I think that Mommy considered them her babysitters and would try to catch a nap when they were outside with us.

Also, my first summer brought Tweek into my life. He was a large cat called a Maine Coon. He was much older, a couple of years I think, and he quickly became my mentor. Because my humans worried about me and wanted me to have a safe place to go, they bought me a small house and put it under their front porch. Tweek saw that I was a little confused about what was happening, so he went inside the house and laid down on the bed they had put in there for me, then came out so I could give it a try it. I think my human has included a picture of me in my house. (Am I cute or what?)

Zeus (also known as Daddy)

*****

It is now eight years later and I have a new igloo-style house.) The porch above my house had railings that had a mailbox for the humans on one rail, but on the side next to the door, Tweek and I used to spend a lot of time just lying therelooking at each other or trying to see what my humans were doing inside. One day we were a little bored and Tweek decided to let the humans know it. He stood upon the rail and put his front paws on the glass door, then let them slide down. Well I guess my humans were impressed, because they immediately came to the door to look at us. Needless to say, when I want to go inside (which is where they feed me now, since they are afraid other cats will try to steal my food) all I have to do is scratch at the door and one of them will let me in. But you know, for some reason they seem to get upset when I want to come inside at midnight, or even 3:00 in the morning. They stay up all night too...don't they? Some humans believe that we cats are supposed to sleep 16 to 20 hours a day. That's only four to eight hours awake to do everything we have to do.

Tweek

My first house

Do you have any idea how long it takes to lick yourself clean, chase mice and squirrels, patrol my territory, and still have time to eat all the goodies put out for me? What is a cat to do? In eight hours? Give me a break! You know, they had a hard time trying to get my mommy to come inside. She did a couple of times, but wanted to go right back out, especially if they tried to shut the door. Now, me...that's a different story. I do like it inside. It's warm, there's even a sofa to sleep on (if I can get my human mommy to vacate a particular cushion), and there's always food and water in my dishes. And best of all, all I have to do is roll over and I can automatically get a tummy rub. I must take after my mommy on that. She was going to have kittens during my second summer, and one day when my human started to give her a tummy rub, my mommy just couldn't get enough. (See the photo here.) They have tried to get me to use a litter box, but no thanks. I did it twice (there was a huge blizzard and I couldn't get out the front door so I didn't have a choice.) I am really an outdoor cat, and I intend to stay one. My human daddy says that I think he's my slave (getting up to let me in and out all the time), but isn't that what humans are supposed to do. So what if I have to come in for a snack every hour or so, I guess that's why they started saying, "there's a cat at the door", when I scratch to let them know I'm there. There's just something about being outside...a sense of freedom. Yes, I could leave anytime; but why would I want to? They are good to me, they feed me, and I get tummy rubs...what else could a kitty cat ask for? My humans have bought me lots of toys. They even took an old fishing pole and put a toy on the end of the line and throw it across the yard so I can chase it. Isn't that nice? I am eight years old now, and don't chase things like I used to, but I do enjoy a good run now and then. Besides, I have to humor them, don't I? Yes, I am very independent; but I also know who takes care of me. They are good to me (even when they take me to that place called "the vet"). I know they love me. I get hugs and kisses (yecch), but I put up with them. I just hope the other neighborhood cats don't see it. How embarrassing! I do have a reputation to keep up. But that, again, is another story.

Tweek and I on our railing.

Chapter Two

THE CAT ON PATROL

Hello again. If you have forgotten (and I don't know how you could forget me, the perfect cat) my name is Aphrodite. During my life with my humans, I have dedicated myself to making sure that no other cat becomes a part of their lives.

Many other cats have tried to make their homes on this end of our street, but none have stayed very long. And that is because of 'yours truly'. My humans belong to me...nobody else. I will permit them the occasional 'oh you're pretty' when they see a new cat or kitten in the neighborhood, but that's as far as it can go. This is MY territory!!!

For example, there was once this kitten that moved into the neighborhood and was adopted by the family across the street. As a part of keeping the other cats away, I must patrol my territory. My humans have a corner lot, so there is plenty of territory to manage. And it has kept me plenty busy.

There have been a couple of non-attached male cats that tried to take up residence here. They even tried the romantic premise, like I would fall for it. I do have to admit that Hephaestus and Phantom (as my humans called them) were both very handsome males. I just could not let either of them get the idea that they could just come in and take over...me, my territory, or my humans.

They called her "Princess". Now it didn't take long for my humans to spot her. (I found out she had been named "Princess".) After a while, I kept wondering why they would sit in their car for a long time when they came home from the store. I mean, shouldn't they be taking **MY** cat food inside?

Then, one day I jumped up onto the hood of the car and when I looked inside, there it was...the betrayal!! My human Mommy had Princess on her lap...in the car! So that was how they did it. They would park the car, open the door on the side away from me and let HER inside. How could they?!! Well, I put a stop to that. When they would come home, I would go to the other side of the car and make sure that SHE would get nowhere near the car. I don't know what happened to her. I know the people were staying somewhere else for a while, so maybe they took her with them. All I can say is, "I hope you're happy...somewhere else."

My humans seem to really enjoy sitting on their front porch swing in the summer time. You don't know how many times I have had to keep a passing feline from coming over to try to make friends. Sometimes I pace back and forth, or even lie in wait, hiding under their truck, which my human mommy used to park right in front of the swing (now, Daddy parks his car there). Just let those other cats try.

The one thing I wish is that they would stop letting other humans come in and stay...for hours on end....even overnight. It's hard enough to guard them from the neighborhood animals…I also have to protect them from other humans. Granted I have to do it from a proper distance. Like outside…from under the neighbor's porch. As a part of my patrolling, I have found that I can use the family car. When sitting on the vehicle, I can see the entire area…nothing will get by me. I also will place myself under the vehicle at times. Nobody can see me and if a certain stray comes by, I can be on them before they know it.

Recently there was a yellow tabby that decided he wanted to try to stake a claim to my yard. Poor fellow. He learned soon enough, you don't mess with "the neighborhood terrorist". At least that's what my humans have started calling me. (Maybe they should have called me "Xena" Warrior Princess!) You should see me in action. No one stands a chance when they come up against me. Sometimes they will hear me during one of my 'confrontations'. Mommy always has to come out and pick me up, wanting to make sure I am OK. She has yet to find a scratch on me. Hopefully, some day she will learn. After all, what kind of impression does it give to my adversary (if he stayed in the area), when I am picked up and cuddled. I have to maintain my reputation, don't I? They might get the idea I'm soft and try to come back again. Well, if they try, I will have to show them again not to mess with the Neighborhood Terrorist.

As you can see, I am not happy being cuddled when other cats can see me

And now to another of my duties….the occasional field mouse that gets into the home. I remember one evening I was 'cat-napping' in my bed, when my human mommy said, "Aphie!". Well, what she didn't know was that I was already aware of the intruder. Needless to say that within seconds I had the little creature, and was happily 'taking care of it' on the front porch. For some reason, they have a problem with my having my 'live' dinner in the home. Like all dutiful felines, I make sure I share my catches with them. I have to make sure I compensate them for the financial burden they have taken on when they purchase my cat food.

They are gracious enough, but never seem willing to let me bring my gifts inside. Oh, well. It just leaves more for yours truly.

The front porch is also a good observation point.

But, you know they do feed me well. I'm not ALWAYS hungry (like my human daddy seems to think). One night my mommy saw a mouse in the kitchen. She felt it was her duty to advise me of it. Can you imagine...she picked me up and carried me into the kitchen and sat me down in front of the mouse?. Now really...I am a huntress, I will stalk when I get ready to stalk. This was downright embarrassing. I don't kill for the pleasure of it...I only kill to satisfy my hunger. And I wasn't hungry. So, naturally, I went back to my bed. You should have heard her laughing as she told my daddy what happened. You know...I still don't know what became of that mouse.

I guess I'd better go now…so many mice...so little time. Be sure to go to the next chapter as I explain how I live life as, "The Cat on the Edge"

Just taking a break in my writing.

Patrolling my territory… camouflage is always advantageous.

Chapter Three

THE CAT ON THE EDGE

Hello again. If you have forgotten (and I don't know how you could forget me, the perfect cat) my name is Aphrodite. I am now nine years old. During my life with my humans, I have been involved in some pretty precarious situations. I guess things have turned out a lot better than they could have, seeing that my cat mommy and daddy were homeless at the time.

Through the years my humans have provided my basic needs: food, water, etc. But when it comes to protecting my territory, I have had some formidable opponents. There was one yellow fellow recently that was determined that he was moving in. I showed him who was boss, and he hasn't been around lately. I know of at least two occasions when my humans ran outside when they heard the fight. Of course, my humans had to pick me up and make sure I was OK...of course I was...I am the "Neighborhood Terrorist". There have been other cats that have attempted to take root here, but to no avail. I have been too smart, and tough, for them.

I like lying on the 'edge' of the sofa.

When not out patrolling my territory, you can usually find me stretched out on the family sofa or across the living room floor. Talking about living dangerously, can you imagine what it's like to be nice and comfy, all stretched out when suddenly there are footsteps and someone is stepping over you. Both of my humans have trouble walking sometimes, and yes, they have accidently stepped on my tail or my paw. They always apologize and give me cuddles (yuck), but I just wish they would be more careful. I really shouldn't tell tales on myself, but I have been known to roll off the sofa when sleeping or playing with a toy. Such humiliation, but it does seem to amuse my humans and I guess I can let them have a little entertainment at my expense (after all they buy my food). BUT NOT MUCH!!!

****

Five years later...

My 'former' spot on the bed,

Yes...It's been awhile since I last picked up a keyboard to write something, but I have been so very busy trying to take care of my humans. One had a bad fall, breaking an arm and leg. Then the other got very sick and ended up in the hospital; but it seems like they're <u>finally</u> a lot better. You don't know how hard it's been to have to human-sit; you know, keeping them in bed or on the sofa resting. The only time they should have to get up is to feed me or let me outside to 'patrol' my territory. Yes, they're still complaining when I have to go out at midnight, then 2:00 am, then 4:00 am? After all, I still have to keep the other cats away from here. I know I am older now (will be 14 this spring), and although I'm not winning ALL of my battles, I do have a certain reputation to maintain. I do have to admit, though, my humans have tried their best. I have heard them asking each other if I am outside, or inside, because it was so cold. Guess, I'm doing my job right…just keeping them on their toes.

I must tell you something about my new bed. Anyway, it's a type of bed that Mommy put on the foot of her bed. It looked really strange, and I wasn't sure about it, so I stayed away. The other morning, while she was getting ready for work, my human mommy decided to sprinkle a pinch of catnip on the new bed. I must tell you, my nose started twitching and I couldn't wait to get onto that bed to check it out. Well, it could very well become my new favorite thing. Hey, Mom…don't forget the catnip tonight!

*****

I am fifteen years old now, and I have been sleeping on the bed with my human mommy. She has given me the whole side of the bed…plenty of room to stretch out. I even have my own little sleeping pad that keeps me warm. My human daddy has to sleep sitting up, because he has breathing problems, so he is in another room.

Every year they take a short four day trip, so one of the neighbors feeds me. He's really good to me, too. Makes sure I have food and water. I have to stay outside during this time, but it's in the summer, so I'm not cold or anything, and I still have my little 'hut' to go into. I am a little troubled, though. I have heard them talking about taking an additional trip…a long one next summer…ten whole days. What will I do? I know the neighbor will take care of me…but it just won't be the same.

So many worries for such a little one like me. I do have to say that the vet…a nice lady, but I hate going there…keeps telling my mommy that I am healthy and doing fine. All I can do while I'm there is hide my head in the curve of Mommy's elbow. Hey…if I can't see it…it won't hurt me. Right? I really hate it when I have to get what they call 'a shot'. I don't care what they say…it hurts. I get back at my mommy, 'tho…when we get home, I make sure I don't socialize with her for at least a day.

Our new home.

*****

Well, like I said, my human mommy and daddy took their 10 day trip and found a beautiful home in...FLORIDA! It's really nice, but I am having a little trouble adjusting. I haven't been able to go outside since we got here. They're waiting for the backyard to be fenced in and some 'pet doors' to be added. They tell me that I will be able to go outside whenever I want once that is done.

*****

Well...they DID IT! They 'adopted' two new kittens. They say that they did it to help them when their other family couldn't keep them. Well, OK...but did they have to bring them here! I mean, this is my house. Granted, it's big enough for all of us, but it's still, MY HOUSE. I've already had to put each of them in their place, but I haven't signed a truce yet. We will have to see about that. I have my own room now... and what they call a twin bed, all to myself. Mommy moved into a larger room that, I admit, does seem to be better for her. She wanted me to come sleep with her there, but I just couldn't do it. And now... the 'intruders' are in there with her sometimes. What am I to do now?

Our new cat tree.

Apollo

Well, anyway, Mommy took me to a new doctor and she told her that I needed some new medicine. I'm not sure I like all this stuff. The dry food is OK, I guess. And, at least, the new medicine is put on my ears instead of me having to eat it in my food...they said I wouldn't taste it, but I can tell you, I did. Oh, in case you're interested, here are a couple of photos of the intruders in my house. I guess they're cute, but REALLY!

Starbuck

It's been three weeks since they 'moved in'. I guess things are getting a little better. Starbuck just seems to say, "oh, she's here again," when I come into the room. I don't think Apollo is quite sure what to do, but he isn't pushing it, too much; so I guess I can tolerate him...to a point. I do have to

admit that they are really just kittens...ten months old now. And so much energy...there are times that I could swear that Mommy was watching the Daytona 500 being played out, right here in the house. Things are slowly becoming tolerable, but those two just have to stay out of my food dishes... they have their own! Mommy does try to keep them away from them and does scold them, but, you know, the 'neighborhood terrorist' just might have to show herself again.

OK, maybe they aren't so bad after all. This morning Mommy brought out a new toy and they were having a lot of fun playing with it. I decided to join them and we actually played together for a few minutes. I used to have a similar toy at our old place, but this one looks a lot neater. Ooops...what am I saying? Playing with the boys. I realized what I was doing and headed back to my room. I hope this doesn't get out. It could ruin my reputation.

Speaking of playing with the boys…if you can call it that…our mom took us all to that vet place again today. I'll admit, I did almost smile when I realized that they were getting shots and I wasn't. At least I thought something was going right until the vet got my mommy to agree to let them do some lab tests on me. *Betrayed again.* The doctor said that I still need to have the medicine Mom tries to give me, but I still don't have to like it…and I let her know at every opportunity. I see her coming with the bottle and I dive under the bed. At least, it works some of the time.

You know, I'm beginning to wonder about these boys. Today, while I was trying to catch a little cat nap on the living room floor, one of them (I think it was the one called Apollo) sneaked up behind me and tried to sniff the tip of my tail. The indignity of it! Well, I showed him when I jumped up, swung around, hissed and swiped my paw at him. Maybe that will teach him some manners. You should always ask a lady cat's permission before sniffing her tail.

The weather here has been quite nice the last few days, and my humans have been letting us go into our backyard. They had it totally fenced in so we would be safe, and I think I'm going to like it out here. There are lots of places to explore, even if I do have to share the space. The old yard wasn't anywhere near this size.

The boys have finally found the bird house that was here when we moved in. I can't help but laugh when they try to climb the pole and the little birds, (bluebirds, no less) dive at them, making them run into the house for cover. I mean, 12-pound cats running from a few ounces of feathered fluff!! They're going to give the feline species a bad name.

My humans have been saying that the rest of our stuff has been pulled out of storage and is being delivered here in a couple of days. I am NOT looking forward to the disruption. I just hope they get things put away fast. I'm getting too old to put up with this madness. It seemed like it took 'furevvvver' to get the house in shape after we moved in.

Well, the stuff is here. So far, it hasn't been as bad as I expected. They are leaving most of it in the garage and bringing in only a couple of boxes at a time.

Another morning with the 'vet'. Mommy was worried because she thought I wasn't walking the way I should. The doc took some pictures (she called it radiographs) and said I have something called arthritis in my hips and lower spine. I guess that's to be expected when you get to be my age. They are trying to decide the best route of pain medication for me. I sure hope it helps.

The boys and the bird house…

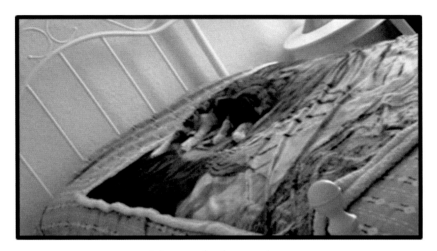

My new bed… yeah…

Since we've been here, there have been a lot of people coming and going. Mommy and Daddy hired a nice lady to clean the house every other week. I know it helps Mommy because she can't get around too well sometimes. The only problem that I have is with this 'machine' the lady uses. I think it's called a 'vacuum cleaner'. Well…that thing is loud. It seems like wherever the boys and I go to hide, it always finds us. And you know the worst part…Mommy and Daddy are laughing at the way we run around, trying to get away from it. Now, I ask you, is that nice? One of the other people that comes is what they call a 'handyman'. I like him. He's really nice, but there are times when he's using what he calls a drill, or a hammer…well it's enough to give a cat a headache.

Well, the results are back, and my test results are back to normal. My mommy has been giving me some medicine in my treats at bedtime, and I do think I'm feeling better. I don't hurt as much. I believe she thinks she's fooling me by putting it on my treats, but I can tell the difference. Oh well…I'm feeling better so, I think I can live with it. I even felt like playing with one of the toys this morning. Besides … getting treats in bed…what's so wrong about that?

Oh, well…got to go. So much to do, so much to explore, so much to eat…another great day!!!

The End….?

In Memoriam

Just so our readers know…a short time after this book was originally sent to the publisher near the end of 2018, we lost our dear Aphrodite to heart and breathing problems. It hurt so much to lose her; but we know that she is no longer hurting, and is running around the fields near the Rainbow Bridge.

Thank you, from both of us, for reading this, we hope you enjoyed it.

Darla Vasilas

Printed in the United States
by Baker & Taylor Publisher Services